HEAVEN AND MIRTH®

Elijah
Prophet Sharing

AND
OTHER BIBLE STORIES TO TICKLE YOUR SOUL

by Mike Thaler

Illustrated by Dennis Adler

*Equipping Kids
for Life*

A Faith Parenting Guide can be found on page 32.

For Jeannie Harmon
who always has a good word,
patience,
and love.
Mike

Faith Kids® is an imprint of
Cook Communications, Colorado Springs, Colorado 80918
Cook Communications, Paris, Ontario
Kingsway Communications, Eastbourne, England

ELIJAH: PROPHET SHARING
© 2000 by Mike Thaler for text and Dennis Adler for illustrations

Published in association with the literary agency of Alive Communications, Inc.,
7680 Goddard St., Suite 200, Colorado Springs CO 80920.

Edited by Jeannie Harmon
Design by Clyde Van Cleve

First hardcover printing, 2000
Printed in Singapore
04 03 02 01 00   5 4 3 2 1

ISBN: 0-78143-512-9

Letter from the Author

Taking this opportunity, I would like to share with you how this book came about. Born sixty-two years ago, I have been a secular children's book author most of my life. I was also content to have a fast-food relationship with God from the drive-by window. At the age of sixty, I came into the banquet by inviting Jesus Christ into my heart. Since then my life has been a glorious feast. These stories are part of that celebration.

One night I sat and watched a sincere grandfather trying to read Bible stories to his squirming grandchildren. I asked him, "Aren't there any humorous retellings of Bible stories that are vivid and alive for kids?" He rolled his eyes and said, "This is it." The kids rolled their eyes, too.

This made me sad, for the Bible is the most exciting, valuable, and alive book I know—as is its Author. So I went into my room, with this in mind, and wrote "Noah's Rainbow."

Since then God has anointed me with sixty stories that fire my imagination and light up my heart. They are stories which, I hope, are filled with the joy, love, and spirit of the Lord.

Mike Thaler
West Linn 1998

Nuggets from Goldie the miner prophet:
"It's Never Too Late to Eat Right."

Author's Note

I have conscientiously tried to follow each story in word and spirit as found in the Bible. But in some cases, for the sake of storytelling, I have taken minor liberties and added small details, such as using an elephant instead of a ram in the story of Abraham. I pray for your understanding in these instances.

4

Elijah
Prophet Sharing

Ahab WAS ONE WHALE OF A BAD KING.
But his queen, Jezebel, was a real orca!★
They deserted the Lord God
and started having a Baal.
This made God very angry.
He sent Elijah,
His number-one prophet
and weatherman,
to give them a forecast.

"No rain for three years,"
he predicted.

This is not good news in the desert.

★ A killer whale.

Ahab and Jezebel thought Elijah was all wet,
so God told him to leave town
and go hide out in a little ravine.

**"There's a water fountain there,
and I've ordered the ravens to feed you."**

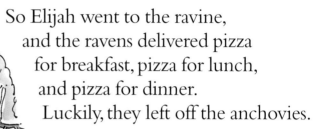

So Elijah went to the ravine,
and the ravens delivered pizza
for breakfast, pizza for lunch,
and pizza for dinner.
Luckily, they left off the anchovies.

But eventually the fountain dried up,
and Elijah got tired of pizza,
so God told him to go to Zarephath.

**"I've made a reservation for you
at a nice little bed and breakfast."**

So Elijah obeyed God
and went to Zarephath.

At the town gate he met a widow
who was gathering twigs.

"Would you bring me a little water?" he asked.

"Sure," she said.

But as she was leaving he added,
"Maybe you could bring me a little piece of bread with it?"

"OK," she said.

"And maybe a small bowl of soup to go with the bread?"

"Uh, OK."

"And maybe a green salad to go with the soup?"

"What kind of dressing do you want? French, Italian, or blue cheese?"

"Do you have oil and vinegar?"

"Sure, anything else?"

"Well, maybe a steak and a baked potato."

"How do you like your steak?"

"Medium, but not overcooked."

"Sure."

"Anything else?"

"Maybe a little dessert."

"Listen buddy, my son and I are starving to death.

7

We're down to our last apple pie."

"Well, God said
you should give it to me."

"Anything else?"

"Maybe a scoop of vanilla ice cream."

"We only have chocolate."

"OK. Do this and God will give you
and your son food till it rains."

"What's the weather forecast?"

"No rain for three years."

"It's a deal."

So the widow went home and fed Elijah,
and the ravens started delivering pizzas
to her and her son every day.

Eventually
her son got sick
of so much pizza
and died.

"Oh," wailed the widow.
"He had one slice
too many!"

"Give me your son," said Elijah.
He picked up the boy and carried him to bed.

"Oh, Lord," cried Elijah,
"Bring this lad back to life."
The Lord heard Elijah,
and the boy woke up.
He blinked.

"I'm hungry," he said.
"What's for dinner?"

"Pizza," said Elijah.

The boy
fainted again,
but did not die.

THE END

Nuggets from Goldie, the miner prophet:
"If you give a prophet a cookie, life becomes a piece of cake."

For the real story, read 1 Kings 16:29—17:24.

Daniel
God's Graffiti

WHEN BELSHAZZAR
became king of Babylon,★
he was not very wise.
He didn't feel that he needed
either God or Daniel
to run his kingdom.
He was a real regal reveler.
A professional party animal.
They called him
"The Belshazzar of the Ball."

One night he invited a thousand
of his closest friends for a barbecue.
He wanted to impress them,
so he got out his best plates—the gold ones
that had been stolen from God's temple in Jerusalem.

★pronounced babble-on

In the middle of the party, something very weird happened. A giant floating hand started writing words on the wall that no one could read or understand. Needless to say, this put a big dent in the conversation, and the king got very scared.

He immediately summoned all his wise men and wizards, who hurried in, looked up at the wall, and scratched their heads.

"It's lowercase," said one.

"It's cursive," said another.

"I saw a sign on a wall once that said 'No handball playing,'" said a third. But none of them, no matter how long his beard was, could read it. Belshazzar got even more frightened.

Then the queen had an idea.
  "There used to be a real wise guy named Daniel
    who worked for Nebuchadnezzar.
      He knew God, interpreted dreams,
      and could spell *Nebuchadnezzar*.
      Let's send for him."

  "Anything," said Belshazzar,
    who was now hiding under the table.

    When Daniel entered the hall,
      the king said to him, "Yo, Daniel,
    where you been keepin' yourself?
    Listen, if you can read the writing on the wall,
  I'll invite you to *all* my parties from now on."

"That's OK, King,
   I'm usually in bed by nine,
      but I'll tell you what
         the writing says for free."

   "Great, great!" said the king,
feeling a little better.

   "It says 'eeny meeny
      miney moe,' which means
         'No handball playing' . . .
      just kidding.
      No, it really means
         'God is very annoyed
            with you, and
      He is going to kill you
         and give your kingdom
            to the Medes and Persians.'"

   "Boy, you're a real
      party pooper!"
whined Belshazzar.
   "I'm sorry I invited you."

   Just then the combined Mede and Persian armies
broke down the door, marched into the hall,
and slew Belshazzar.

His last words were,
   "The only thing worse
   than party poopers
      are party crashers…" THUMP!
      "You've got to hand it to him,"
      quipped Daniel.
      "He threw parties to die for."

      "When we have a barbecue,"
      said all the Medes and Persians,
   "we'll use paper plates."

THE END

Nuggets from Goldie, the miner prophet:
"God can cut any ruler down to size."

For the real story, read Daniel 5.

Elisha Traps Blinded Arameans Out of Sight!

Now the King of Aram
made war on Israel.
He kept setting traps
and ambushes,
but Elisha kept warning
Israel's king,
who would avoid them.

The King of Aram
got really bugged.
"He knows everything I do—
there's a traitor in my army."

"No, my lord,"
said one of his generals.
"It's that prophet, Elisha.
He has ESP or CNN
or something,
and he knows everything
you think or say."

"I think I'm going
to kill him,"
whispered the king.

"He knows it,"
whispered the general.

So the King of Aram took his army
and surrounded Elisha's house.

"What shall we do?" cried Elisha's servant.

"No problem," smiled Elisha, stepping out the door.
And when the servant looked,
he saw that Elisha was protected by a circle of fire.

As the Arameans closed in on him,
Elisha prayed to the Lord,
"Strike these men blind."

And in an instant they were all
bumping into each other.

"You guys got the wrong address.
Follow me and I'll take you to Elisha's house," said Elisha.

So the army all joined hands
and Elisha led them right into the midst of Israel's forces.

"Shall we kill them?"
asked the King of Israel.

"No," said Elisha.
"We'll get them
seeing-eye camels
and white canes
and send them all home."

So it was that the King of
Aram stopped raiding Israel's
territory. Although once a year
he did ask for a donation
to buy crossword puzzles in braille.

THE END

Nuggets from Goldie, the miner prophet:
"When God is on your side, your back is covered."

For the real story, read 2 Kings 6:8-23.

19

Shadrach, Meshach, and Abednego

Real Cool Cats

NOW, SHADRACH, MESHACH, AND ABEDNEGO
are three pretty famous guys.
They rank up there
with Manny, Moe, and Jack,
and Huey, Dewey, and Louie.
And the way that they
became famous
is a pretty hot story.
It happened like this . . .

When old King Nebuchadnezzar put up
a ninety-foot, fourteen-carat, golden godlet,
he decreed that whenever
any of his subjects heard the sound
of the horn, flute, zither, lyre, harp,
bongos, bagpipes, and kazoos,
they should fall on their knees
and worship his pretentious, precious pile.
If they didn't fall down,
they would immediately
be thrown into
a blazing furnace.
Now, Shadrach, Meshach,
and Abednego
were nice Jewish boys.
There was no way
that when they heard
a dance band, they were going
to fall down and worship
a glittering, glitzy glob.
When Nebuchadnezzar
got wind of this,
he got hot under the collar
and summoned them.

He said, "Shadrach, Meshach, and Abednego,
if you guys don't fall down
and worship my Tiffany Epiphany

when you hear the horn, flute, zither,
lyre, harp, bongos, bagpipes, and kazoos,
it's into the fiery furnace with you."

"Oh, Nebuchadnezzar," they replied,
"whether we fry or fricassee
is up to our God, the Almighty."

"Well, we'll just see,"
said Nebuchadnezzar,

23

and he ordered the furnace turned way up high
and commanded his soldiers to
throw in all three guys.

Now, that furnace
was so hot
that it burned up the soldiers
on the spot.
And when Nebuchadnezzar
looked in,
it singed the hairs
upon his chin.
But right in the middle,
walkin' around
were Shadrach, Meshach,
and Abednego,
and someone else
they had found.

"Hey," said Nebuchadnezzar,
"these guys are really cool.
I think I'd better change my rule."

So, he ordered them out,
'cause they were *rare*,
and he fell on his knees,
deep in prayer.

And ya know, when they came out humming
  "There's Gonna Be a Hot Time in the Old Town Tonight,"
they didn't even smell of smoke.
They took the whole thing as a joke.

Nebuchadnezzar
was really impressed,
so he wrote a new law
which was his best.
  It said that God
    had passed the test
    and came out
      far above
      the rest.

Then they had a barbecue,
  and he made Shadrach, Meshach, and Abednego
  his three fire chiefs and gave them red chariots
  with lots of lights, bells, and horns.
  For their God was *asbestos* there is.

THE END

Nuggets from Goldie, the miner prophet:
"If you play it cool for the Lord, He'll get you out of hot spots."

For the real story, read Daniel 3.

26

Abraham and Isaac
That's My Boy!

MORE THAN ANYTHING IN THE WORLD,
Abraham wanted a son.
When he and Sarah
were newlyweds,
that's all they prayed for.

"I hear ya," said God,
**"and I promise you
a bouncing baby boy."**

But the years passed,
and the cradle stayed empty.

"Nu already, God. We're almost senior citizens."

"Patience, Abraham, patience."

So more years passed, and the only thing that increased
were gray hairs and wrinkles.

"God, I'm getting too old
to coach Little League.
When's my son coming?"

"Patience, Abraham, patience."

Finally, when Abraham
was one hundred years old,
and Sarah was ninety,
they had a bouncing baby boy.
They were tired, but very happy, and were featured
on the front page of *The National Enquirer.*

Abraham named his son *Isaac,* 'cause he joked,
"Boy, was *I-sick* of waiting for you."

He and Isaac
did a lot of things together.
They spent days at the
Senior Citizens' Center,
and rocking on the
front porch of their tent.
Every Wednesday night
they played bingo,
and every Saturday night
they played checkers.

Life was great, until one day God sent Abraham a telegram:

ABRAHAM GO TO MT MORIAHS TOP STOP
AND SACRIFICE YOUR SON ISAAC STOP

So Abraham, who was obedient to God,
put his son on a donkey and headed for Mt. Moriah.

"Where are we goin', Dad?"

"Well, Son," said Abraham, with tears in his eyes,
"we're going to make a sacrifice to God."

"What are we going to sacrifice, Dad? A dove?"

"Bigger," sobbed Abraham.

"A lamb?"

"Bigger."

"A calf?"

"Bigger."

"What then, Dad?"
asked Isaac.

"The biggest sacrifice
there is in the whole world, Son,"
cried Abraham.

"Well," puzzled Isaac,
"God knows where we're gonna find an elephant?"

When they climbed Mt. Moriah,
Abraham built an altar and put his son on it.
He took his knife out of its sheath.
Isaac trusted his dad. And his dad trusted God.

Suddenly, God sent a singing telegram,
ABRAHAM STOP STOP DON'T DO A THING STOP
BECAUSE YOU WERE WILLING TO GIVE ME YOUR ONLY SON
I AM GOING TO GIVE YOU AS MANY DESCENDANTS
AS THERE ARE STARS IN THE SKY STOP

And when Abraham dried his eyes,
he saw an elephant
stuck in a nearby thicket.
He and Isaac went over
and put the elephant
on the altar,
which flattened it
completely.

So Abraham
named the place
The Lord Will Provide.
And Isaac pretty much
worked it out later
in therapy,
although he didn't give
good Father's Day gifts
for years.

THE END

Nuggets from Goldie, the miner prophet:

"God doesn't kid around."

For the real story, read Genesis 21:1-7, 22: 1-19.

HEAVEN AND MIRTH®

Elijah
Prophet Sharing

Age: 6 and up

Life Issue:
Having faith in God and His Word
will help us make right choices.

Spiritual Building Block:
God's Faithfulness to Us

Learning Styles

Help your child learn about God's faithfulness in the following ways:

Sight: If your child has a children's version of the Bible, locate and read one of the stories from the Bible text. (The reference is given at the end of each story.) Talk about the character(s) in the story. How did they show faithfulness and obedience to God? How did God help him?

Sound: Read each story aloud to your child. In what ways did God demonstrate His faithfulness in these stories? Why? It is God's character to show His love for us by protecting us from harm and providing for our needs. Ask: How does God take care of us?

Touch: How do we demonstrate faithfulness to each other? Talk to your child about being consistent and loving to friends and family. Stress that being faithful means to be there for someone when you feel like it and when you don't. What are practical ways that your child can show God's love to others? (Examples: send a card, offer to water someone's flowers, carry groceries from the car, etc.) Plan to do several things with your child to help him or her understand this principle.